The Yellow Sweater

The Yellow Sweater

Poems by

Margot Wizansky

© 2023 Margot Wizansky. All rights reserved.
This material may not be reproduced in any form, published,
reprinted, recorded, performed, broadcast,
rewritten or redistributed without
the explicit permission of Margot Wizansky.
All such actions are strictly prohibited by law.

Cover image by Harold Gould, 1936
Cover design by Sasha Wizansky
Author photograph by Helen Feinberg

ISBN: 978-1-63980-410-8

Kelsay Books
502 South 1040 East, A-119
American Fork, Utah 84003
Kelsaybooks.com

*To Florence and Harold, my parents,
who taught me about love*

Acknowledgments

I acknowledge, with gratitude, the editors of these journals where these poems first appeared.

American Journal of Poetry: "My Father Never Told Me"
The Aquifer, digital edition of the *Florida Review:* "My First Time"
ArliJo, Issue 164 (Gival Press): "The Lessening," "One Night in San Miguel"
Baseball Bard: "If the Goddamn War Hadn't Happened"
Cimarron Review: "The Bathrobe" (appeared as "An Early Case, 1961")
The Healing Muse 23: "Like a Museum the Day It's Closed to the Public"
New Ohio Review: "A Race Car Made of Sand"
Tar River Review: "Jello," "Borscht"
Think, Volume 13.1: "The Black Slacks" (appeared as "Shopping for Black Slacks")

Deepest gratitude to my husband, David, and Sasha and Ben for their loving support.

My bottomless thanks to Barbara Helfgott Hyett, my teacher for twenty years, without whom this book would not have come to be.

And thanks to my poetry cohort for helping me refine these poems: Cynthia Bargar, Wendy Drexler, Vivian Eyre, Xiaoly Li, Steve Nickman, Sarah Snyder, Heidi Dube, John Heavey, Susan Pizzolato, and Elizabeth Sylvia.

Contents

One

The Yellow Sweater	15
If Time Could Flow Backward	16
If the Goddamn War Hadn't Happened	17
Formal as a Royal Palm	18
A Race Car Made of Sand	19
A Door in the Wall	20
My Father Never Told Me	21
My Father Learns to Cha Cha	22
Tiny Onions, Olives, Green Cherries, Twist of Lime	23
Father in Necktie at the Fountain of Neptune	24
His Offering	25
New Boots	26
What We Once Found Essential	27
In the Doorway	28
Poem with a Line by Lucie Brock-Broido	29
Family Slides I Haven't Seen for 50 Years	30

Two

Smells	33
Borscht	34
Jello	35
The Mirror	36
Breakfast	37
In the Retirement Home	38
Flash and Interval	39
An Early Case, 1961	40
Good Sleep	42
Bergman and Bogart	43
At 90 My Mother Found Love	44

Like Moss on a Rock	45
The Black Slacks	46
Bracelet	47
Tinsel	48
My Mother Became Holy	49
The Lessening	50

Three

The Servant Call Button	53
Braids	54
Love You Like That	55
Where I Come From	56
Danger	57
Grounded	58
Tryouts	59
My Old Friend Has Died	60
I Didn't Know the Earth Was Dying	61
Kitten up a Tree	62
Lucky	65
One Night in San Miguel	66
My First Time	67
A Real Romance	68
Love According to the Arc of the Sun	69
Traveling	70
Summer of Love	71
House Blessing with Roses	72
I Can't Help Watching You	73
On Your Birthday, I Buy You a Table Dancer	74
For I Consider My Husband's Bald Head	75

Four

Epithalalium	79
Lamentation, Interrupted	80
To My Husband, Going to Bed	81
Fifty Years On	82
Ode to the Enemies in My Garden	83
Tethered	85
In Isolation, I Watch the Film, "Emma"	86
Loving	87
Exaltation	88
First	89
Darkness Breathes and We Dance	90
Like a Museum the Day It's Closed to the Public	91
Answers	92
I Googled Coma	94
Your Kind of Singing	95
A Couple	96

One

The Yellow Sweater

My mother was late
to Life Drawing
the night she met my father.
The only empty space
was next to him, so she
set up her easel.

Sidelong, the whole evening,
he watched her
yellow sweater.
She drew her nude,
a line faint pink
between each toe.

His nude was verdigris.
He spent a long time
on the innuendo
of breasts.
He didn't bother
with a face.

If Time Could Flow Backward

My father would still dance the two-step
in new cowboy boots he bought at the shop in the square.
Everyone would eat the picture-perfect turkey

I'd roasted, and we'd listen to Frankie play cello
in the living room. The twenty-two pound tuna,
untaxidermied, unglued from the plaque

commemorating the only prize my father ever won—
would swim off Miami, the hook unhooked from its mouth.
If time flowed back to our house on Ott Street,

to the Chesterfield chair he collapsed in every night,
post-heart attack, the upholstery would be taut as the day
it was new, and his fake gold watch, for the twenty-five years

he worked at Sure-fit Slipcovers, tucked into its velvet-lined box,
would go back to Girard-Perregaux, the time before
his children disappointed him with our separate mistakes,

our first disagreeable mates, our salvage operations.
My father's ashes would gather themselves
to fly out of the Caribbean where Mother cast them

off Grand Anse beach, cruise back to New York
aboard the Ocean Pearl in a cardboard box,
his bones rattling all night.

If the Goddamn War Hadn't Happened

Goddamn war. If my father hadn't worked nights at the shipyard.
If he could have used his education in the Law.

If he hadn't had to help in the family business, medicine
cabinets. If that family business hadn't gone under.

If his father hadn't died so young. If my grandmother
hadn't married again, left him alone to fend for himself.

If he hadn't traded Xerox too soon. If he'd forgiven himself.
If he'd moved us to a big house on Lehigh Parkway.

If my mother hadn't clicked down the stairs in high heels,
Chanel Number 5, a backless dress for the cocktail party.

If not for my father's leaky heart. If he could have spent his days
trolling for tuna on the deep and warm and boundless.

If the Phillies ever went all the way.

Formal as a Royal Palm

They hired a woman to watch us
and flew off to Havana, where
the Hotel Nacional's gilded grandeur
was peeling away, and it was always
nighttime in the bar. Years later,
in deep dementia, my mother
remembered the way escorts in cocktail dresses
sat on stools under chandeliers low
enough to be their hats, veiled in smoke
from the salesmen's cigars. My father
took his dark rum straight, strolled
with my mother on the Malecón,
a fashion runway cooled by sea spray.
She wore Dior. In his dark suit,
he was formal as a royal palm,
before the music crept away to hide
in alleys and the satin voices went back
to shining shoes for a living, before
the embargo sent all the salesmen
home stateside, before Havana's
resplendent days turned sick at heart.

A Race Car Made of Sand

Everything made my mother nervous:
the baby crying, sand on the floor, the flies.
So we went out to the beach.
I took my bucket and shovel.
My mother sat my little brother up on her shoulders
and carried the towels and a canvas chair for my father,
He'd had a heart attack and was too weak to carry anything.
He wore his cabaña suit, light green with white palm trees,
his legs, pale like the hotel room sheets.
He hadn't shaved.
His face had been bluish for weeks,
the circles under his eyes, dark as his beard.
Mother said I was too heavy to sit in his lap.
All afternoon I dug a string of frantic little ponds.
Nothing was right: my back was sunburnt;
my father hardly moved.
Uncle Robert came on a bus from the city
to build me a race car of sand, with jar lids
for hubcaps and for headlights, clamshells,
and he found a quoit on the beach for the steering wheel.
He dug me a driver's seat that just fit,
and a rumble seat for my little brother.
My father peeled me an apple with his penknife,
in one long piece that didn't ever break.

A Door in the Wall

My father paints a miniature,
a grid of stars on a night sky, dark
      indigo without menace
           no cold breath insinuating

everything else dazzles like grass—

four minarets against the sky

one spire a Coptic cross,
one, a Christian cross,
a fountain, a tree,
      red, blue, yellow, blue—

and in front a lion stands guard,
      for the tail and mane my father
unraveled string, and the lion looks straight out,
wide-awake with a half-smile, almost human,

my father's painted a door in the wall, shut tight,
      too small
           even for death.

My Father Never Told Me

The year of his Bar Mitzvah his father died suddenly.
Things he didn't talk about. He never sang again, only
whistled sometimes. His mother remarried the plumbing
supply king, who refused to have teenagers in his house,
so she left my father and his sister alone in the apartment.
Did his mother come back to wash his clothes, put up dinners
while her new husband sold cleanout plugs? Her death
certificate says divorced, but when, what grounds? He must
have gnawed on her absence in that cramped apartment,
must have taken it to school, let it lunge after him
on the playground, his fifteen-year-old face already
shattered with new beard, his shirts unironed,
no forgiveness in him, holding onto the hurt that grew
while he sat bitter on his brown-tweed chair for the rest
of his years, listened to the days dwindle down
to a precious few, dead at fifty-four, just like his father.
Oh, his stuttering heart! He never told me how bad it was.

My Father Learns to Cha Cha

In our town every house had its arsenal
of bar tools, every time of day
its own drink. My father, home from work,
was a dry martini, pin-striped

suit swapped for shirt and chinos, cheeks
shadowed from supervising the day
shift, sofa covers cut and stitched,
and I was young enough to believe

we were a couple, and so I taught him
to cha-cha to his Cuban LP, his name
scrawled on the cover, right over the breasts
of the woman in white. Silent but never

distant, he was Old Spice, gin-breathed,
his hands resting light on my sparrow shoulders,
each big ear half a Valentine,
lifting his sorrow, my slippers

balancing on his loafers. When I fell off,
he'd stop, pick up his martini
coastered on the coffee table and drink it down.
No dips. No leaps. No twists or sweat—

too hard on his heart.
We crossed the room
in small increments, *no me molesto
si tengo cha cha cha*. I counted for him.

Tiny Onions, Olives, Green Cherries, Twist of Lime

Every weekend in the 1950s,
my parents drank to the chatter
of ice in the shaker, a martini
with a tiny onion, green cherry,
twist of lime, or one of the twenty-five
other cocktails my father
could shake by heart.

He'd add the merest breath of vermouth,
hold the olive on his
cocktail fork until the brine
drained off, the perfect host,
never asking, Would you like
another drink, as though
he might be counting.

Sylvia's here. *Poor Sylvia,* my mother
always said, Morris' wife, who started
on Gilbey's and tonic at 10 AM,
one after the other, all day, all night.

When I walked through the living room,
their friend Marty called out to me,
Hey, you got the rag on?

I tried to run up to my room,
but my mother was sitting
on the stairway laughing,
holding a cocktail. Down
the front of her little black dress
was someone's hand,
and it wasn't my father's.

Father in Necktie at the Fountain of Neptune

If he were any more formal,
    he'd be a statue, too, stiff, buttoned up
        in this photo in the faded glow
            of Palazzo della Signoria. He'd promised to send us
                a photo of Michelangelo's David,

yet after he planned this trip all winter long,
    it seems he settled for lesser beauty, the sea-god
    and his six-pack, each muscle row its own dark shine,
    curly hair like my father's,
        who clasped his hands over his midsection
            as if to hold his own body together,
        a body he didn't think much of,
            hated to see in photos.

            He only wanted to photograph Mother
        in designer clothes before the wonders of the world,
and here he is, by himself, handkerchief folded
        in his jacket pocket, 1950s tourist,
    his back turned to naked Neptune and the satyrs,
        unsmiling, weary, disappointed by travel.

His Offering

He just keeps on in the muck,
the concentrated muscle of his silence,
bent over the bull rake—the whole sea
radiating from where he stands,
the bottom sucking at his feet.

If only he'd show me how to walk
the quahogs up, place my feet next to his,
toe the round firmness—not a mudder
but the heft of a living shell,
its rock-tug resistance against my hand.

Oh, if he would only shuck one—
his square-nailed fingers
shaped like mine, part
the shell, unbind the marrow,
offer it to me, gray and glistening.

New Boots

Today it's all Elvis on my car radio
singing "Proud Mary," in his seamless
voice, the range and ache of it,
those urgent depths and the delicate
upper register, that song playing when
my father danced for my mother
breaking in his new Western boots,
sliding the square toe, tapping
the slant heel, kicking sideways
in a back-to-his-roots Russian move,
kicking away his bad heart,
the crazy boss he hated,
swinging his white handkerchief
over his head until he dropped
dead, the handkerchief floating
slowly to the living room floor.
The record kept playing *workin'*
for the man every night and day,
until someone came and clicked it off.

What We Once Found Essential

My father loved to be where the sea dazzles
        and the sun sets brilliantly at martini time.
                This year it's a cold season—wind destroying
        every mark woman or man has made.
The sky is busy—clouds blow by so fast it feels
        like the earth is speeding.
What we once found essential is inside out:
        hairdos, umbrellas,
              eating with friends.
Wind roars like grief, gathering all
        the intervening griefs,
              rolling toward me.

The time I should have been happiest—the day
        my son was born—I imagined my father
              looking down at him,
and the day turned bittersweet.
        My son would never know this grandfather-love,
no trips to Florida for spring baseball,
        no careful analysis of his golf game,
The advice I didn't get from him—cars (lease, don't buy),
        Money (be cautious),
              he would have warned,
        though he wasn't.

About love he didn't have to tell me anything.
        The way he looks at my mother in the last photo
              of the two of them before his sudden death,
        her head in his lap on the sofa,
her eyes closed, his hand resting on her heart.

In the Doorway

My father's ghost showed up
at my bedside when my pregnancy
bled out, to take my pulse, dressed
for work in suit and tie.

Sometimes, he appeared
in my dreams, dying.
I sat with strangers at a séance
to summon him.

I wanted him to tell me
what happened after he left.
Was he traveling?
Could he see the future?

Would I ever have a baby?
Would I?
One evening my daughter felt a breeze
on her neck, looked up to see him

smiling in the doorway, just like
the photo on my desk, in a cardigan
and Phillies cap, and when she turned back
to her homework, he was gone.

She wasn't afraid, she said,
though she was sure
no one would believe her.
It took years for her to tell me.

Poem with a Line by Lucie Brock-Broido

The very drawer of salt and ache and rendering,
memory of my father, its separate parts,
taken each by each, and not the whole

the memory close to me, close when I am
in semi-isolation. How he too limited himself,
in fear for his heart, some days hardly moved

stayed in the drawer of his safety, his big heart weary,
only a few steps into his dance it took him down
big wheel keep on turning

heart must have been worn down by blood on his platter,
the raw beef he ate

young enough, his hair hadn't gone very gray, still
curly, those curls he kept clipped lest someone mistake him
for a Mediterranean fisherman

though the clip exposed his ears, those big friendly ears
he hated

and the salt, salt of his humor, never mean but wry
and unexpected

no jokes about mother
and we weren't to laugh either—
most nights she lay awake listening for his breath

the ache he must have felt, always, the ache for what
he didn't have—his father died too soon

and rendering, the wings of love he gave, in his quiet,
and I was sure of it

Family Slides I Haven't Seen for 50 Years

Between a smile and no smile, beginning
and end of a blink, my father's eyes half-closed,
black sweater vest, dark checked shirt.
My mother, black dress and little cocktail hat,
their eyes with the same crinkle, their mouths, love.
In the next image, they're laughing, mouths
the same curve, a study in black. When we
were alone, he broke out and told me a hard truth.
I'm afraid to go to sleep. I might not wake up.
Every-night all-night fear I understand.
My father appears damaged, unfocused,
caught by a photo that stops time
for a millisecond between the cracked panes
of his life. Perfect sync they were, so full of laughter.

Two

Smells

On hot days, my mother splashed herself
with chilled cologne from the fridge.

Your scent is your signature, she told me,
you announce yourself when you enter
a room, and you aren't completely dressed
until you perfume yourself
in all the right places, a subtle but haunting drop
on the inside of your wrist in case someone
kisses your hand, a daub under each ear,
for a kiss on the neck, and between your
breasts, for what, I didn't know,

and when she was ready for a cocktail party,
my mother came downstairs in a cloud
of Estée Lauder Youth Dew,
a lingering musk, in a black dress,
a long string of pearls, patent leather
ankle strap heels with their tiny buckles
and I said, *I bet you think you look nice.*
I could make her cry.

Borscht

As though she hadn't stopped cooking years past,
                 when forgetting turned dangerous,

my mother makes borscht today with her whole body bent over:
    boiling the beets, running cold water over them,
            skins slipping right off,
       marrying the peeling, shredding slurry with her fingers,
the return of the broth,
              stirring in sour cream last
                    for that otherworldly magenta,

slant sun spinning her hair,
          a cloud of filaments. Oh my heart!
                Dust motes lighting her way—

just stand here beside her at the stove—
        the salt and sugar
               a kind of passing—

Jello

My mother could suspend
a sparkling afternoon, cast anything
in jello—ubiquitous side dish,
her vegetable, and since success
depended on following the rules,
she accepted the challenge—
the science of suspending
bing cherries in a red field, cucumbers
floating in a sea of green cream,
a structure for boiled eggs.
Oh, how proud she was to add
extra gelatin, cut and stack blocks
extra-hard and durable
for the children, in colors
nature never intended.

The Mirror

My mother draws thick black circles
around her eyes with a smudgy pencil

and makes her entrance into the living room,
prancing around as though she's at summer camp.

A dazed raccoon, I'm thinking. It's late
in her life, and I can't bear it.

I hold a mirror to show her what
she looks like, but she won't focus.

My mother, who believes the unaccessorized
life isn't worth living, hasn't lost that impulse,

but today her swimsuit sags and her beach
cover-up is stained with lunch. I ask, *Mom,*

may I take off your make-up? and I wipe
the black circles off her face. She lies down

on the sofa in the midst of her children. She's asleep
in seconds, her breath a peaceful rumble.

Breakfast

Steak. Luscious, blood-rare. Eggs
over easy. At the damask table

my mother and I watch Grant,
straight-backed in his wheelchair,

dapper in a moss linen shirt, take
the tubes from his nose, drape them

across his chair as though oxygen
were a fashion accessory, gaze

at the voluptuous body of the woman
getting coffee, pouring cream,

the skin of her arms, the flanks of her legs,
her platform shoes, her tulip skirt.

He brought last night's steak, uncooked,
to have it grilled this morning

and now he carves it
along the grill marks. The last

of the sirloin bows to the last of the yolk.
How better to count out the days?

In the Retirement Home

Do not speak of slow interment.
The residents could lose a day hunting

a piece of paper. They pluck at themselves
in the manner of the senile.

Their backs round more and more.
Outside, late magnolias, extravagant

as ballgowns, blacken in sweet decay.
No one notices this quick birth and death.

And memory is an exhalation. They have
given up each other's names—

friends of their waning, friends
of their splintering. None of them

wants the startle of spice in their food
or heartbreak or grief's perfume.

Flash and Interval

Down. The night pours, ponderous.
Sea, breaking itself
until she can't follow
the tide in its turn and rivulet.

Sea, breaking itself,
becoming her penance,
the tide in its turn and rivulet,
pitiless, miserably shedding,

becoming her penance,
flash and interval, warning her,
pitiless, miserably shedding.
As though she's bound, hand and foot,

flash and interval warning her,
oh God—she might piss herself—
as though she's bound, hand and foot,
her bed, unwashed, clothes un-ironed,

she might piss herself. Oh God—
where is the Light?
Her bed, unwashed, clothes un-ironed,
how will she wash herself?

Where is the Light?
If she can't follow it,
how will she wash herself
down? The night pours, ponderous.

An Early Case, 1961

Mother's elegance, her fashion sense—
Christian Dior suit and pillbox hat,
her buying trips to Paris, her talent
for selling cocktail dresses to the rich,
amounted to nothing the night her boss,
widower and sole owner of that flagship
department store, a palace, antiques
everywhere, crystal chandeliers, white-gloved
atomizer women spraying French perfume,
and in the café, drinks two jiggers strong,
whipped cream five inches high,
invited her to dinner and she, expecting
the other buyers for drinks
in his suite at the Waldorf-Astoria,
knocked on his door. He was alone,
wearing horn-rimmed glasses
and a bathrobe, nothing else.
She thought she'd interrupted his shower
until he untied the bathrobe, let it hang
open, and made her a proposition:
divorce your husband, marry me,
and your children will want for nothing.
Her broad smile dimmed and she composed
herself, took her leave, trying not to register
shock or offend him. Still, the next day
he fired her. Your performance, he said,
and for fifty years, she never told anyone,
even after she was scooped up to run
another fancy-dress shop, even after
my father died without kicking that man's
sorry ass, even after Anita Hill testified.
Well turned-out at 90, wearing a silk scarf

and three necklaces, still believing she'd
asked for it somehow, Mother told me
for the first time about the miserable sandwiches
her boss had ordered in that night for dinner,
white bread, buttered, with a little slice of ham.

Good Sleep

My mother said she never slept.
She always slept. On the very edge
of her bed as far away as she could get

from her second husband. In places
intended for wakefulness—in the library
on a bench, or in a chair where she could

disguise her dozing. She gave herself to sleep.
In the first-row orchestra at "Much Ado."
In front of the giant TV in the lounge,

the Phillies night game grinding down,
until the security guard woke her,
walked her back to her apartment.

A wakeful night after a day of many little sleeps.
In the morning asleep when her gentleman
called to be sure she'd made it through,

and when we drove her from Philly to Boston
for the holidays, six hours in the back seat,
asleep, such a good sleeper, my mother.

Bergman and Bogart

In the retirement home, they might be
Bergman and Bogart—her white hair, mantled

in chiffon, his trench-coat collar, over wide.
They lean into each other, delicate,

bittersweet, shy. On their bench,
they do not touch, her face regal,

his long throat. They nod to me
going by, as if embarrassed, even here,

by their coupled conversation
after the concert, after the café.

He'll walk with her as if in some
European city, amid last century's upheaval,

as though they'll soon be parting,
as though they won't.

At 90 My Mother Found Love

He gentled her as one might coax
an elder dog. Her cheeks blushed for him.

When she came alone to breakfast,
he'd set a place for her, a sweet roll,

every day the same. Little revolver,
a Smith and Wesson, sequestered

in his drawer, he showed her once.
She didn't know she had been his time-

of-not-killing-himself though he had the grace
to hold fire until she'd left to visit me.

To their acts of love I'd been witness:
hand touching hand, hand

touching knee, his kiss shy
on her forehead. She'd tilt

her head up to him
the way dry grasses lift to rain.

Like Moss on a Rock

Safe with a talisman around my neck, a pearl from a quahog
in a little golden cage, sorrow covers me like moss on a rock.
Is this the way my mother readied herself as she began
to lose her body's dignities? Dressed in her fuzzy leopard vest,
had an aide fasten her necklaces, two or three of them,
open the curtain, fill the room with warm light,
then to breakfast, half a grapefruit, a small container
of peanut butter, a spoon to eat it with, a cinnamon roll.
As I wake, I think about breakfast the way my mother
taught me, the same sequence every day, eggs, scrambled
in Irish butter, eaten from a blue willow plate, salmon bits,
mushrooms, onions, a cup of foam-topped cocoa.
Every detail pre-arranged, no decisions at the last minute,
I've put on quiet clothes. I study the willow plate.

The Black Slacks

At the boundary waters of her decline,
my little mother decides she needs new black slacks.
So thin from salting her food, forgetting to eat,
I'm trying to find her what fits.

My little mother's decided she needs new black slacks.
In the dressing room, she holds a pair in her hands.
I'm trying to find her what fits.
She can't remember if she's about to try them on

or take them off, the pair she holds in her hands.
She knew retail, high end. It was her life.
She can't remember if she's about to try them on,
slacks on the floor, on the chair, lopsided on hangers.

She knew retail, high end. It was her life.
Soon we find a rhythm—I hand her a pair—
slacks on the chair, the floor, on lopsided hangers—
she tries them, rejects them, I whisk them away—

soon we find a rhythm—I hand her a pair.
After she tries them, I give her another.
She tries them, rejects them, I whisk them away.
These fit! she says, the very pair she wore this morning.

I'm finished giving her another pair to try.
So thin from salting her food, forgetting to eat.
These fit! she says, the very pair she wore this morning
at the boundary waters of her decline.

Bracelet

In the hospital, she wears bracelets,
I.D., the D.N.R., drowning her
in all the rivers of all her lives.

She looks toward the mountain,
bare of snow and says beautiful,
without seeing.

I smooth the bruise on the back
of her hand, wipe her mouth
where it drools, give her a hairbrush

and she brushes her silvery waves.
When I drape a silk scarf
around her neck, she ties it artfully.

I tell her about her stroke,
tell her where she is, make her
say it to me, say it back, tell me

she's there, and from somewhere,
her voice, tiny gravel, *If anyone calls,
tell them I won't be in to work.*

Tinsel

In the dining room, the aides set the tables.
No food smells, no food colors.

Patients sit in wheelchairs. I sit quiet on my stool.
The new-age TV plays sunrise, waterfall, sunset.

A woman makes a little lamb sound, her hair
brown lambs wool. Another sings "This Little

Light of Mine" in a voice like tinsel.
More waiting than eating, though someone

feeds herself a mash of peas and carrots with a spoon.
And in that garble, I feed my mother, who loves

coffee ice cream most of all. I yell ice cream!
in her bottomless ear. She presses a sippy cup

hard against her forehead as if it were her mouth.
I take it from her—it leaves its mark.

My Mother Became Holy

In assisted living, my mother strips down
to holy, memory reversed, and her vision,

a cloudiness that can't be corrected.
She stops weeping, comes to live

where lost is charming with her luminous
waves of hair, five necklaces, five bracelets, five rings.

One is beautiful, five, even more.
The gardener gives her a Calla lily,

the manicurist orders Timeless Pink,
and the night nurse walks her outside

in her nightgown to see the moon. New friends,
elders with their wits about them,

talk to her when she no longer sees or hears,
leaving offerings: sacramental cards

and votive candles. They come as pilgrims:
Peggy pushing a walker, Mary, her oxygen tank,

Margy of the constant tremors, who touches
my mother's face with dancing hands.

The Lessening

Her face pared down to fine armature, she is not
exactly sleeping, deeper than sleep, more
regular. I count her breaths, forty-eight
a minute, inconsequential to the air.
Her every breath a labor of purpose,
not struggle, even though her eyes
are shut and her mouth's been
open for days. I can't resist
touching the sweet radiant
whiteness of her hair. The
trinity of heart, lungs,
brain, winding down,
her chest lessening,
impossible to
measure what
I have left of
her, she who
made me.

Three

The Servant Call Button

The little rise under the rug her guilty secret.
It would be bad manners not to keep
her hands on top of the table.
My grandmother's foot fiddles with it.
She buzzes Queenie from the kitchen,
can't be ignored, whine at her ear—
soup's too cold! Queenie doesn't have
a last name, or if she does, Nana
never uses it. I call adults Mr. or Mrs.
if they're not in my family.
Why is she only Queenie? Nana
complains about her as though she can't
hear—she puts too much salt in everything!
When Queenie makes chicken soup,
the smell of singed feathers lingers.
Nana puts all our old clothes in brown
paper bags, insists Queenie take them home.
My mother tells me she hates the button,
hates the way Nana treats Queenie,
but around Nana, my mother's quiet
as a toad. On Sundays, Queenie's
day off, we go to Nana's for brunch.
I serve bagels to everyone from a basket,
the only time I'm allowed in the kitchen.

Braids

My mother wanted me in braids
every day when I was a little girl.
She hurt me with my hair.
I counted the black and white
hexagons on the bathroom floor
while she sliced a part
down the middle of my scalp,
yanked those braids
tight as though she hated
the beauty of my hair, thick
tumble of it, the dark sheen,
as though my hair were
dangerous when loose.
No strand could escape,
my slim braids ensnared
by rubber bands that pulled
hair out when my mother
unbraided them at night.
I wanted a peek-a-boo wave
like Veronica Lake, wanted
to feel my hair blowing
behind me as I rode my bike.
I paid the price for closeness
while my mother wrestled
with my hair, subdued it.

Love You Like That

Mother at the beach, her swimsuit
au courant, the stripes curving around her breasts,
shields her eyes from the sun, not looking

at me in back of her in my navy wool swimsuit,
a little white anchor attached to my flat chest.
I could be burning up in the sun or walking too far

away down the beach and she's locking eyes
with the photographer, my father, who loves her
so much. When you're old enough to know

you can't have your father, don't you want someone
to love you like that? And what kind of mother
did you want, a peacock of a mother, strutting

her feathers, the most beautiful clutch of them,
or only a little mother, a hummingbird, darting into
the torenia to taste the pollen, not lingering, just checking

on her flowers, a mother who'd lie down on the bed
with you when you were scared at night, unmoored
in a vast sea of dark shapes writhing undefinable,

lie down with you until you fell asleep, a mother
who'd tell you how beautiful you are, changing
into a woman before her very eyes, a woman like her,

who'd protect you from boys who noticed, a mother
who'd answer her phone at five in the morning,
listen while you cried your heart out, love you over the phone?

Where I Come From

I come from under the lilac tree where Stevie and I
        showed each other our bottoms all afternoon
        and my mother never saw,

from the backyard willow I mourned when a hurricane snapped it,
from the tree I climbed to read in at the farm,
from my father's come-home whistle blocks away,

I come from every dog who disappointed me—
        Spotty who loved next-door-Barry better than he loved me,
        Nicki who came with distemper and died,
        Holly with a bowel problem who was "taken to a farm,"

from neighbor boys who wrecked my clubhouse
from Lanny who aimed his gun at me loaded with birdshot,
and from teachers who knocked our knuckles with a ruler.

from years of trouble falling asleep, so small in the vastness,
from *you-don't-know-the-value-of-money,*
from 25 cents a week allowance and steak so rare it was purple,
from teasing that pokes at you where you're most ashamed,
        your duck feet, your breasts that keep on growing,
from my best friend's noisy house—homemade pita,
        Tom Collinses, and pinochle after school.

from my father all my friends loved
        and the wives of my parents' friends loved,
        and Annie in the office at the slipcover factory
        who knitted him argyle socks every winter.

from the stink of the Toni Home Permanent my mother gave me
        so I could have curls like hers
        my mother, who told me *always cater to your man*
        and read aloud to me from *Poems to Read Aloud:*
        I will arise and go now . . .

Danger

after Tova Friedman

We stumbled into a dark. Into a dark.
Mud sliding our feet. Thorny
underbrush grabbing our ankles.
Boys, neighborhood boys, in those innocent woods,
sitting on wooden crates they hauled in,
sitting beside oily black water, maybe a swamp or a pond.
Could have been cottonmouth snakes.
Could have been swamp rat swimming.
Could have been raped.
Could have fallen and disappeared,
no streetlights, no buildings to get our bearings,
giddy from the secrecy, giggling,
drinking near-beer with the boys
showing off their private secret high,
not fallen boys, just boys showing off,
not touching, not sex.
It wasn't danger. I didn't know danger.
The barracks.
Nazis stomping big-black-boots, danger.
Your mother made you hide
under a woman just dead, warm at first,
you so small and still. Still. So small.

Grounded

Something mean I did to my little brother, no doubt,
        so awful I was at fifteen. My parents
                grounded me for two weeks, beginning the first day

                of the Allentown Fair. I didn't dare sneak out while
        they were at work—that much obedience
left in me. Friends came to my bedroom window

and I had to tell them. How I'd miss the midway,
        games of chance I'd never win,
                like Ball in the Bucket, stuffed animal prizes,

                even the freak show, people with too much hair
        in the wrong places or tattoos all over,
back when that was freaky, the tinkly music of the calliope

I'd long outgrown, and the stale smell of popcorn, a whiff of dung
        from the 4-H tents and corn dogs, sausage, fried dough,
                food that gave me low-grade nausea,

                aggravated by the rides, the terrifying Round Up
        I wouldn't have to ride, whirled high and pinned us against
the metal cage with centripetal force while the bottom dropped out.

I tried everything, pushed myself to be brave, never admitted fear.
        Mostly we wandered the fairgrounds to see which boys
                from our class were wandering, too.

                The fair was magic, lights so bright everything
        just outside the grounds was thrown into deep darkness,
where the carnies lived in caravans, I imagined, ready to move on.

Tryouts

The Wing twins were on the football team, Tommy and Mikey,
a different species, gangly, walking down my street, leaping up
to grab tree branches. Clyde, too, my boyfriend until
his mother discovered who I was. Nancy, blond and blue-eyed
with her shapely legs, was certain to be captain of the cheerleaders
and didn't even really care. She coached me, her small dark
skinny friend, for the tryouts. I dreamed of being with
the popular girls, their blond hair in crisp little dips
over their foreheads. I wanted that pleated skirt, canary and blue.
had the cheers down pat, war chants, *Hit 'em again, harder!*
the arm movements, fists in the air, synchronized kicking,
nothing very callisthenic, except for the cartwheel, a leap of faith
I couldn't take—throw myself in the air and come up smiling.
Couldn't make the squad.

When I turned forty, I draped myself in a sequined red bra
strung with beads, a gold-threaded chiffon skirt I'd made,
and I assembled my friends to watch me belly dance.
I'd mastered the Turkish Drop, a small miracle. It was a perfect
performance. I was standing upright one second, then I arched
my back, folded, and dropped flat on the floor. Wild cheers!

My Old Friend Has Died

I wouldn't even dress for school until
I knew what Nancy was wearing.
We egged each other into small
delinquencies, hid our neighbors'
lawn ornament—ceramic sleeping Mexican,
spiked our Seven-ups with whiskey
after school. We laughed nonstop
at everyone else, mean and gasping,
smoked Winstons and played Pinochle
in the basement. I bet my baby-sitting money,
fifty cents an hour. In the laundry room
we took turns necking with our boyfriends,
hated our mothers in vicious,
bottomless need. Nancy's father was
a martinet in his tiny kingdom.
He said hardly a word to her,
then disappeared forever. My father
showed us how to make Tom Collinses,
didn't even need a bar guide. We giggled at his jokes.
We went on to fall into heart-blinding,
reckless, stupid love. Nancy held that part
of who I was. She took my history when she died.
I don't know what to do with hers.

I Didn't Know the Earth Was Dying

Nothing was perishable, nothing was
miraculous to me, either, not even the sun,
its multiple orbs illuminating every living thing,
trees lifting their branches to meet it halfway,
cabbages, rolling their roundness toward it,
the deep abiding sun I knew nothing about
in my twenties, hardly looked at, shades drawn,
could have been shining or not, and I missed
the brushstrokes of all the starry nights,
focused on that great burning in my center,
a mystery interesting only to me.

I wasn't singing to an abundance of world,
didn't detect any force or light.
I wrote a little at the edge of things,
couldn't move past the turmoil in my head.
Is a poem a kind of litany?

Was it only once, when I was a girl,
that I skated to the outside of town
on a frozen stream, miraculous, ephemeral?
I looked down at fish and leaves frozen
together under clear blackness.

Kitten up a Tree

i

He wasn't like the college boys in my life—
he was sure what he wanted. Me. He didn't say love.
I don't even remember the sex, except that he demanded it.

Your little boy body, he said.
Less than 100 pounds then,
with all my parts and they weren't skimpy.
Your whiskers, he mocked me, though
I didn't have any.

I needed to understand his beauty.
He wasn't responsible for it.
His face was symmetric like a fox.
Eyebrows more pointed than arched.
A swagger in his walk.
Didn't look at me from inside his eyes.
I was a cold reflection off the surface.

His namesake, the blue jay, wild, gorgeous,
mean, thieving, and cheating.
He played trumpet—the embouchure on his upper lip bee-stung.
Sometimes that scar bled. Hard tones, blasts of notes,
flames of notes, the sound pressured, not a delicate melody.
What it's like when art hurts, when you can't lose yourself
in the music, can't give pleasure with your grace.
When his band worked bars, he sometimes sang Misty,
helpless as a kitten up a tree. He never sang to me.

The only book he read when I knew him:
History of the Peloponnesian War,
battle after battle, Thucydides' copious detail.
Those epic battles seemed to soothe him.

ii.

My mind blurs when I try to go back
to those burnt stalks of my history
to remember why I married him.
I'm a city of fog. I can't remember wanting.
Or decay. Or gravity like a bright star. And oh, God, I ran away
and married him as if I wouldn't have another chance.

I waited a few weeks to hurt my parents,
pummeled my father with one more heartbreak.
How could I know he would be dead in five years?
Marriage. A small space I inhabited then, lived indoors,
never using any large muscles, unacquainted with the ocean.
Didn't walk in the woods.
I kept painting landscapes and apples.
Smoked, but let the cigarettes burn down in the ashtray.
As if I had all the time in the world.
As if, at twenty, my time was running out.

He kept a photo of his stillborn daughter in his wallet,
proof of virility, said nothing about babies in our time together.
Can I say together?

iii.

Back in West Virginia, they'd called him Junior.
I was a way out. My father helped. Computers,
early days. A local bank put him in charge.
He was small change.
I didn't believe he was cheating on me with a woman from work,
till he brought her to a party at our place.

Once I made Caesar salad.
Why did you make that salad? I won't eat it.
He threw it at the wall.
Dressing dripped down behind the phone bench.

He slashed a portrait of me by a former boyfriend,
a nude torso, impasto, green. It didn't even look like me.
He chased me through the kitchen, the bedroom.
He could have killed me.
I locked myself in the bathroom.

Living with his unholy voice, like bombs overhead,
like a parade of knives, a constant elegy.
He was always leaving fast, tire marks on the driveway,
the light crushed, and still a veil.
The Austin-Healey he insisted on, small,
fast, like him, top down, the engine sparking,
loud combustion, drunk, head-on.

Lucky

I saw the wrecked car and screamed.
Only one scream in me. I couldn't cry for him,
not for sadness—that never entered into it,
not for shock, the blue fire of that car crash

more inevitable than shocking,
his drunken spinout, his head
caved-in, his matinee-idol
looks wiped out.

He threatened me, *Cook just like my mother
or I'll throw it out,* nothing green,
fatback and navy beans I couldn't call food.
Those dark smoky bars where I watched him

while his band played and drank too much,
no one in those joints really listening. Disembodied
years, narrow and broken. I was dazzled for awhile
by his handsomeness, his music—must have been why

I ran off with him. When people came to call on
the grieving widow, no one knew what to say.
I couldn't speak truth, tell how relieved I was.
The end of his life, the beginning of mine.

There must have been a funeral, a cortége I can't
remember. A few months later, his family came back
for the body, took him home to West Virginia,
where someone might have dropped by his grave.

One Night in San Miguel

In the ex-pat bar I met a Texan
with a three-day stubble
and no last name, lanky
and laconic, his legs
long as my margarita,
and in that one inebriated hour,
everything was reckless
and I couldn't get my bearings,
went off with him
to a hidden hot spring
utterly obscured
in sulphur mist,
and peeled off
my flowery Mayan blouse.
First I, then he, dove
into the steam
without a thought
for all our possible deaths,
and then we held each other
in some vagrant sleep,
most of my sorrow
still ahead.

My First Time

The memory buzzes under
my skin like neon—in my early
twenties, before I understood
my daily risk of harassment
and humiliation, before I had
grievances, before I knew I was
entitled to grievances, I was
at the gynecologist, wrapped
in a johnny, lying down
on the examining table,
knowing in the observing part
of my brain that a nurse
was supposed to be with me,
afraid of what the doctor
might find, and he entered
the room friendly, an older man,
asked me a few questions,
and then commanded, *Slide on
down here, Margot. I'm gonna
fill you full of cold steel.*

A Real Romance

You take a deep breath, lift me off the chair—
Nina Simone is singing,
and you carry me to your couch.

Sitting beside me, you shyly read me
Prufrock—decisions and revisions . . . how should I presume?
and you hand me a small box you take from your pocket—

I open it—a ring, fire opal on hammered gold,
ask what it means.
Maybe we'll get married; maybe we won't.

A real romance—it isn't joyful,
it's maybe. I'm hot. I'm cold. I close my eyes
to recover—you go into the kitchen.

I hear the can opener and the rustle
of butcher's wrap, probably a small flank,
glistening and lean, the way you like it,

and the thump of the knife on the board
as you cut it precisely, and the sizzle of oil in the wok.
When you're ready, you come to me,
Are you hungry?

Love According to the Arc of the Sun

March is more tentative than vernal,
two steps forward, one step back,

weak winter moon, an icy hill,
and you, sliding in old Army boots,

reticent as a lamb. I wait, kicking
my feet to stay warm.

May, we're blooming, bees in the pollen,
our tent sultry, and even so

I scatter my summer days
in a circle of torpor.

By autumn equinox, we're aligned,
an everyday convenience.

On the longest night, we burrow in,
don't speak of where we've been.

Traveling

I'm sorry I wouldn't let you look for the watch I dropped
at the ballet—no matter how many times I told you I didn't
care about it, you insisted—you were so furious, you walked
Mexico City streets all night. I'm sorry I wanted to leave you
over nothing, really. You and I were still new, two forces
colliding. And I got so sick—traveler's disease, the foul green
of it. Then you were struck, and it brought us back together.
We tore toast into little pieces, fed each other, grateful.

Isla Mujeres, nothing but sand, a half mile wide,
five miles long. We walked to the far end, high noon,
the sun disorienting, atonal brightness searing off the landscape.
How alone we felt, filled with the peace of the world.
We swam in a lagoon with tiny curious creatures:
squirrelfish, striped and spiky, angel fish,
neon blue damselfish. On our way back, we bought
a fat spotted grouper on the dock, its face like a bulldog.

A few boys emerged from the scrub, dug a hole,
gathered bamboo, brought limes, a paste of condimentos,
cooked the fish whole for us. Music wafted
from the Zazil-Ha and we danced in the sand,
laid the fish on a plank, tore at it in firelight,
our fingers and mouths red from annatto seeds,
chilis stinging our lips, all of us feasting
till we'd picked the bones clean.

Summer of Love

Mass General Hospital, 1968

She'd smoothed her white hair to see me,
looked older than she was. She lay there alone,
hardly a rumple in the sheets. I was her social worker,
and as the summer unfolded, sat at her bedside every day

while she told me her life story—married off,
a teen to an older man who sold fruit at Haymarket,
a nice man but distant, focused on his tangerines,
loose skin, easy peel. Five children, scattered now.

Grandchildren. *Some of them I minded while
their parents worked.* Her voice grew wispy,
heart trouble taking her breath. After years of obedient,
perfunctory sex, *he rolled on, he rolled off;*

it was nothing to me, she discovered feelings
down there, an intensity she wasn't explicit about,
how she'd unlearned the language of a man
who knew nothing of touch. I wondered how

a woman could be so disconnected. Those last months
she'd lived at her daughter's in a room off the kitchen.
Delighted for her, I imagined moonlight filtering
through the curtain as she learned her body.

I could have died without knowing, she said.

House Blessing with Roses

After the closing, we exorcised
the old cottage, not wanting
      to sleep with any foul spirits,

          offered a prayer in every room,
the master bedroom where we heard
someone had died, even the open-air shower.

We threw a little of my father's ash in the harbor,
      said a blessing.

I stuck a faux rose tattoo on my shoulder,
        and we decorated the house with roses,
            slow to open, those roses, unkempt
at the end, a little slovenly.

      After the house party, crusted dishes, candle stubs.
We argued whether to leave the dishes till morning.
      The phantoms had been driven out.

He says the work of marriage is boring and he doesn't mind.
      I say I like the tight adherence of it,
          like rose petals that don't show you
their interior until they've all dropped.

I Can't Help Watching You

row the dinghy out, step
onto the toe rail, snap
the pelican hook behind you,

wrap the spinnaker halyard
three times firmly
around the winch barrel.

How exquisitely you trim the draft and camber
of the mainsail until
it responds, tightening

whatever is there
for the taking,
plunge into,

admire the risky angle of heel,
the wind rousing the sails.
I could be that wind,

strum the shrouds, unshackle your
wide-brimmed hat, tangle
your lines.

On Your Birthday, I Buy You a Table Dancer

Her name is Heavenly, and she sits
on the edge of the table in front of us,
so close you could touch her
with your tongue, but you've been told
there's no touching. You sit upright
in your chair, gripping my hand so tight
it hurts my fingers. She wears short shorts,
a t-shirt, oversized and white, "I love Cape Cod"
on the front, pulls it off and lays it on the table,
ready to get to work. Milk chocolate,
her skin, the kind that leaves a slick of butter
in your mouth, her perfume, the tropics after rain.
She presents her bountiful breasts to you,
takes the lighted candle from the table,
lifts the little glass holder head-high,
arches her back and drips candlewax
over one breast, peels it off in a single piece
with exquisite slowness, her smoky eyes
half-closed, humming Jimi Hendrix.
An honest night's work. When she hands
you the peeling, still with its nipple shape,
you take it like a schoolboy, as though this is a test.

For I Consider My Husband's Bald Head

after Christopher Smart

On the pillow, his baldness wrinkles like waves
that come to rest between my ear and my shoulder.
He is not entirely bald. Spiky hairs poke up here and there.
If they were whiter, they would be daisy petals.

Below his eyelids, his eyes are brown and doggish.
His ears, his pleasant ears, widen his smile
and draw my eyes away from his baldness.
He is obliviously handsome.
He is kind to everyone,
but especially to others who are bald.

When he swims the harbor,
his baldness shines and lifts
with every breath of light.

He examines his baldness with rough hands
that polish his boat's bright work.
He washes his baldness every morning and covers it with aloe.

I am his only barber and he lets me paint stars
and stripes on the blank canvas of his head, Inauguration Day.

He wears a wide-brimmed canvas hat stained with summer,
or a wool watch cap pulled down over his ears,
but mostly a red beret, always and only
red, and when he has a scotch or two,
I can grab the stem of the red beret, pull it erect,
and turn it into a pope's mitre—
he is as incorruptible as the pope.

Because he leaves his head bare you can trust him.
For his head is a beacon.
He has never ever considered a toupée.
An honest man will not consider a toupée.

Four

Epithalalium

for Meghan and Ben

Let the feast be salt and sweet, a pungency of herbs,
and you are artichokes, prickly petaled,
cleaned, steamed, choke reamed to the heart.

You are not perfumed-pricy or softening
at the core, but apples, kept ripe by cold,
cooked down, ambrosial, saucy.

Baking is like marriage, constant, not immutable,
as the soufflé puffs itself out of all proportion
or falls in, uncertain, unexplained.

Glean what you need from the family fields—
marriage, the covered dish, holds the aromatics,
even grief and disappointment, savory in the mix.

Deep in the soup of it, the chicken already brined,
let the liquid lift the dumplings
when they're done. Stir, stir, the soup's forever served,

the pot never empties. Sit down together at the table.
Cast yourselves to what you know and what you cannot know.
Cast yourselves to love.

Lamentation, Interrupted

I sat down to write a lamentation
as afternoon cast its long shadow

and painted the sails in the harbor gold.
I began with my youth lost to riches

I held but didn't know: clear eyes, taut skin,
yearning untrammeled. I would never

grow old. And the middle, praise
the middle, when purpose was everything

and took the place of wonder, though wonder
was also there, for later. I thought to end

with sorrow for the lateness of the afternoon,
for the subtle changes that stack,

one upon the other, the very air humid
with sorrow, enclosing me, filling

the rooms, everything made or done
in the service of it or the giving up of it,

but then at my table, they are lifting
the first blueberries to their mouths,

my grandchildren, watching each other
eat the blueberries, humming as they eat,

and I, the witness to such savor,
go early to bed, early rise for more.

To My Husband, Going to Bed

after John Donne

Our bond, our joys, we gave each other
long ago. Warm me gently now.
Full nakedness was once the Paradise
we roved, a fair world we were
licensed to explore. We're no longer
mystic books that reveal
a beauteous grace, but in the dark,
still earthly soft, the looseness
of our skin made softer still.
Off with your cardigan, then,
the elbows patched in suede,
off with your tie, your corduroys,
the pocket shredded
from a giant ring of keys.
Floss with vigor. This is your exercise.
Count your pills out from their cases.
Put on running shorts for sleep,
and I'll wear a long gown with a tasseled tie.
Yet our souls are uncovered
and open, each to the other.
Come, Husband, come,
as the shadows steal in. Hold onto me
as if your life depends on this.
I wait for you, and you for me.

Fifty Years On

Some people thought we were mismatched.
I never mistook your quiet for weakness.
After the baby came, we stopped speaking

for the whole summer. You thought
I had no room for you
and I didn't. On your birthday

I made you a card, painted a big bowl
of strawberries and inside I wrote,
I love you berry much and put it

on your pillow. The silence was over.
We never spoke about it. With the second
baby, it happened that we became a family.

Stalwart, we'd week-end off the grid in a cabin
in the woods. The children swung on vines,
learned stars, toads, and salamanders.

We bought a house, took in our brothers,
my cousins, assorted friends,
whoever stumbled along the road.

Ode to the Enemies in My Garden

Every year I plant my garden with hope,
starter plants, seeds, Thai basil, tarragon,
watch every day for the miracle of sprouts,
do what I think I need to do
to keep my enemies at bay,

drop fox urine from Poland around the perimeter,
hang mesh bags of garlic,
finally put up a seven-foot fence.

They come as if Beatrix Potter had summoned them,
Nutkin or Tiggy-Winkle, carrying a basket
of spoiled gleanings: snap peas, a green tomato
with a huge bite missing, the tender lower branches of cedar,
even new hydrangea buds,

the graceful, feathered, furred, striped, antlered,
the tiny, huge, and in-between,
the bold and furtive, fast, and always quiet,
the flyers, crawlers, amblers.

They don't know mischievous, good, or bad.
They don't know wild food
or cultivated. They don't know
taking or stealing—only eating to go on.
I never see them do it—only a deer
still and staring with her big soft eyes,
a chipmunk scurrying into the stone wall,
a bird on a wire singing its heart out.

The hornworm, the tomato hornworm
stands alone, unbeautiful,
spiral pleated body
hard to differentiate from the stem,

its green color the same
and the tiny thing eats voraciously.
I can hear it chewing.

Praise to my son-in-law who comes running
when I scream, grabs the worm,
squashes it with his foot,
the bright green of that death
splashes his white overalls.

Not a tragedy, the hornworm's death.
Not a tragedy, my garden destroyed again.
They're not taking from my plate.
This is extra for me,
what they need more than I do.
Each plant theirs for the stripping.
I should be consoled.

Tethered

Sadness could be my conjoined twin
or a rough insistent toddler pulling at me.
Maybe I regarded my father
more after he died.
When he was alive,
I never thought about him
as a person, hadn't understood
his disappointments, his sorrow,
his humor or wisdom.
Now he's with me always.
Sadness spills over,
insinuating itself into everything
remarkable in my life,
children's births, grandchildren's,
times I'm seized by longing.
Sadness enhances me,
churns me like the roiling
outside my window,
fierce wind rousing whitecaps
in the harbor. Was it windy
like that the night my aorta burst?
My unexpected survival,
the long crawl back to awareness,
and the full package
of what I had to write.
My almost-death stays with me,
this new part of me
that never lets go.

In Isolation, I Watch the Film, "Emma"

Emma of the golden ringlets rambles
in a woodland with a friend. At the hat store,
she buys a ribbon—hats are so important,
they can double the size of a head.

Emma has been very rude to her neighbor.
For weeks, her insult has hung in the air.
How much those words have stung! She must
present herself. It's the nineteenth century,

and her apology is a basket of vegetables.
She's afraid to say anything. So am I.
If I speak my mind to you, I could destroy
the delicate balance of our isolation.

I stumble through my scrubby garden,
pass the boat shed, the old wooden
lobster pot, eel grass, oyster shells,
mud mussels along the water's edge.

Back on the shell-path, I pick spring's
first daffodil, put it in a vase
of wavy glass, where it glows
more yellow than yellow.

Loving

The tupelos are dancing
as they do every afternoon,
dancing and twisting,
pink-gold on one side
as the sun lowers,
light climbing their trunks
from grass to sky,
pallid, wintry today,
the tupelos reaching out
to each other, this gesture
a gentle foxtrot,
as if they've let go of passion
that could open them
to lightning, open them wide
and vulnerable to wind.
In the obsidian dark,
my legs reach for your
warmth, for the honey
of your skin. Strange
to say skin this old
is honey. We've grown
into each other
through absorption,
taking each other in.
Like the tupelos,
let's dance and curl
around each other
as long as we can.

Exaltation

Every day, the rapture of birds,
sunset approaching in red velvet shoes,
leaving prints where the sky touches water,

that radiance reflecting on the sea's flatness.
Dark blue-violet streaks I want to
plunge my face into. Improbable red

blazes on the west side of every tree. Fades to dusk—
the ordinary story of night beginning.
And soon the moon, the shiver of stars.

Once, in Oxford, I heard the Magdalen College
boy choir, the only time I felt exaltation
in a chapel, those ruby-bright

unbroken voices praising—no matter
who they praised—their clear madrigals
soaring past a multitude

of polychrome saints, scaling the Gothic arches
to a place I'd never been,
a place where I might fly.

First

For whom left am I first?
—Lucie Brock-Broido

Is anyone left for whom I'm first?
Scrawny, jaundiced, my mother's first, I was snatched away,
weaned by force at six weeks old, my mother sick,
her friend took on my howling protests through the night.

Scrawny, jaundiced, my mother's first, I was snatched away.
Could she hear my cries from her hospital bed?
Her friend took on my howling protests through the night.
Our only guarantee—we'll lose the one for whom we're first.

Could my mother hear my cries from her hospital bed?
First for me, my tiny daughter, firefly who hardly roused to nurse.
Our only guarantee—we'll lose the one for whom we're first.
My daughter wailed whenever I lay her down.

First for me, my tiny daughter, firefly who hardly roused to nurse.
Couldn't she grow up fast, be independent, strong,
not wail whenever I lay her down?
First and clinging, she was sailing toward a loss.

Couldn't she grow up fast, be independent, strong?
I couldn't take much needy wanting, holding.
She was first and clinging, sailing toward a loss.
These days he's my first and I am his

but I still can't take much needy wanting, holding.
Weaned by force at six weeks old, my mother sick.
Isn't that what life does, takes the one who loves you best
and no one's left for whom you're first.

Darkness Breathes and We Dance

Beginner's patchwork, my sleep, sections stitched
through the night, the first section with its neat hem,
the second a bit more ragged, and on to uneven
pieces attached with big rough stitches that don't
hold, swaths of time between them.
What wakes me in the night, I hardly know—
you move in the bed, false dawn's birdsong,
a pain here or there. It's still a life of miracles,
breakfast that never fails me, sparkle on the water
too bright to see, a cloudless sky, though tomorrow's
could be mackerel or cirrus, and the miracle of you,
there in the right place, the right time, to save my life.
Then darkness breathes on the window, comes earlier
and earlier to close me in a box, a big one
like a refrigerator carton. Room to move around a bit,
but I can't leave. I dread that delivery. Much as I delight
when leaves turn to butterscotch, always in the back
of my mind, the pall of bleakness to come.
Music parts the dark skies, a celebration of song
to break the solitude, Bruce Springsteen singing
"Thunder Road"—*maybe we ain't that young anymore* . . .
You come to me while I cook, twirl me around
and dance me. It's been so long. The loneliness we share—
our world of simple ritual might break around us,
might turn to sand, turn to night.

Like a Museum the Day It's Closed to the Public

for David

I'll try to tell you why I can't live
in that house anymore since we left
for green untainted space, though once
in a while I visit and hesitate in
the anteroom, take the stairway and
it's neat and organized, wastebaskets empty,
fridge and freezer free of any comestibles,
and in the little cupboard for poets
who won't be gathering here again—
paper, pens, clips at the ready, and I go on
to the hallway I shuffled sleepless nights
with a walker, the corner of the sofa,
where I sat lost in healing, unmoving
for weeks, fearful of trusting my heart,
closed in, autumn fading to the lightless season,
yet enough to make my eyes burn,
the therapist who came to teach me to walk
straight, fry an egg, friends who sat with me
while I drifted off, a husk with nothing to give,
dim life inside my body, and I suffered
my failure to entertain anyone until I felt
my power coming back to me inch by inch.
Our old house looks like a museum the day
it's closed to the public, no one to see
my ocean paintings. Why can't you understand?

Answers

after Pablo Neruda

1.

Why were you searching the house for me?
I woke from a dream and you were gone.

Did a bell ring for you in your dream?
Yes. I worried you were tangled in moonlight's net.

Why did you cry when you told me about the ambulance?
I wasn't allowed to ride with you and I thought you'd die alone.

Why didn't you tell me this story before?
I'd let it vanish with my sadness.

Why do you tell me now?
Your poems bring back everything on the river's currents.

Don't I sleep beside you every night?
You do. I never wanted solitary sleep.

How long will you listen for my breathing?
Forever.

2.

Aren't you recovered?
My body, ninety percent, after the foreign country of rehab.

Why do all your poems end with two frightened lines?
No matter what, I come back to my death.

Why are you thinking about this now?
I wasn't there when it happened.

What do you think about when you read your poems?
How you didn't abandon me.

Does it help you to write about it?
Yes, but then a black crow flies low over me.

How can we get through this?
Watch the hummingbird drink from every flower.

I Googled Coma

Best not to know my chance
of waking from coma was
eleven percent to twenty-four percent.
When I opened again to the bleak
of the world, neither asleep nor awake
for days, empty but for my heartbeat
that's maybe too fast, no color,
not even soft silver of rain, no wish
to see anything, no thirst, no hunger
for food or your hand holding mine
or stroking my hair—your touch
might ground me, but you're a raptor
trapping a sparrow, and I turn away,
making me lonely, both of us lonely,
to get out of bed today my only goal,
to shower while you watch over me,
get dressed, scramble an egg, settle
on the sofa with my urge to be quiet,
not to speak because it's too much effort—
how miserly I am with the spoken word—
and at the same time, you're more vocal,
maybe in reaction—you shout at the radio
in the bathroom or say the obvious,
while I doggedly cling to the flanks of the world.

Your Kind of Singing

No matter what happens, I need you to love me. Need isn't
neighborly. It's rough and it pulls at you, pulls at you, not
a short story of the flesh. It's the map that marks the pain.
Before I met you, I spent my days indoors with friends,
shades down, smoking, playing pinochle. Pathetic. You took me
away to look into the purple hills of the rest of my life. In time
we married. On the way to the hospital in labor, I thought *my life
is about to change and I don't want it to.* The birthing took
so long—that tiny chain of bones resisting. I needed my father
to be a grandfather. He would have known how. I hear you
moaning a sad song with the radio, as though you're wounded
and merging with the sadness. For you, it's ecstatic. My desire is
more than bodily. I want to bind the wound in your soul, always
a stain on your joy goodness can't erase. The mystery of us.

A Couple

after Yang Jian

She's grown old.
He, a bit older.
Days pass quick as a chipmunk crossing the yard.
They eat too fast, saying little to each other.
He has a passion for wind and sail,
throws himself on the wild of the sea.
She prefers to float on warm swells close to shore,
gaze at the dazzle on the water.
It's been too hot to touch each other for weeks.
After dinner they feel the beginning of a breeze caress their faces.
They wait for sunset's performance,
possibility of scarlet, peach, or lavender.
Will it steal away mute
or go down in a blaze?

About the Author

Margot Wizansky's chapbook, *Wild for Life,* was published with Lily Poetry Review Books (2022). Her poems have appeared online and in many journals such as *The American Journal of Poetry, Missouri Review, Bellevue Literary Review, Ruminate, River Styx, Cimarron,* and elsewhere. She edited three anthologies: *Mercy of Tides: Poems for a Beach House, Rough Places Plain: Poems of the Mountains,* and *What the Poem Knows: A Tribute to Barbara Helfgott Hyett,* her teacher. She won two residencies, one with Writers@Work in Salt Lake City and also with Carlow University in Sligo, Ireland. Margot is retired from a career developing housing for adults with disabilities. She lives in Massachusetts.

www.ingramcontent.com/pod-product-compliance
Lightning Source LLC
Chambersburg PA
CBHW030053170426
43197CB00010B/1513